British Royalty Quiz Book

Early Monarchy to the Present Day

by

Joanne Hayle.

Questions – Early Monarchy

What was the first king of England's name?

Ǽthelstan

Egbert

Edmund

Ǽthelred

Where did the first king hold the First Council of All England in 931AD?

London

Bath

Colchester

Exeter

Who is widely acknowledged to have been the first monarch to bestow the title of Prince of Wales on their eldest son?

Edward I

Henry I

William the Conqueror

Richard I

What was name of the King of England who reigned between 978–1013 and 1014–1016?

Edmund I

Ǽthelred II

Engelbert III

Alfred I

Which King sealed the Magna Carta in 1215?

King John I

King Harold I

King William II

King Cnut

What does Magna Carta mean in English?

Great Register

Great List

Great Audit

Great Charter

Who was king of England 23 April to 18 October 1016?

Edmund II

Edward I

Edgar II

Harold II

What was the name of the King who reigned from 1016 to 1035?

Cnut the Great

William the Conqueror

Edward the Confessor

Harold II the Soldier

What was Harold I known as?

Harold Rabbitsfoot

Harold Deer

Harold Harefoot

Harold the Hound

Edward the Confessor was married to whom?

Edith of Wessex

Elizabeth of Mercia

Clothilde of Burgundy

Matilda of Flanders

What the names of Edward the Confessor's parents?

Ǽthelred the Unready and Emma of Normandy

Ǽthelstan the Unready and Emma of Provence

Edgar the Unready and Matilda of Burgundia

Edward the Unready and Isabella of Castille

Who was the last Anglo-Saxon king of England?

Harold II

Harold I

Hector I

Henry I

In which battle did this king lose the throne?

Battle of Westminster

Battle of Bosworth Field

Battle of Cirencester

Battle of Hastings

William II was married how many times?

None

One

Two

Four

William the Conqueror belonged to which royal dynasty?

Norman

Hapsburg

Romanov

Danish

Which date was the Battle of Hastings?

14th June 1060

14th July 1064

14th August 1065

14th October 1066

Who was King of England between 2nd August 1100 and 1st December 1135?

Henry I

Henry II

Edward I

Edward II

Which King followed him?

King Stephen

King John

King Richard

King Henry

What was William II popularly known as?

William The Red

William The Beard

William The Warrior

William The Norman

How many Kings have there been with the name of Stephen?

One

Two

Three

Four

King Stephen's coronation was on which day?

24th December 1135

25th December 1135

26th December 1135

31st December 1135

What was his wife's name?

Matilda of Burgundy

Matilda of Cologne

Matilda of Aragon

Matilda of Boulogne

Eleanor of Aquitaine was married to which king?

Henry I

Henry II

Edward II

John

How many daughters did they have?

One

Two

Three

Five

Who was Henry II's father?

Richard I, Duke of Burgundy

William III, Count of Boulogne

Louis IV, Comte of Brittany

Geoffrey V, Count of Anjou

Who was the King between 6 July 1189 – 6 April 1199 although he was absent for some of his reign at the Crusades?

Richard I

Richard II

Robert II

William I

What was the name of this king's illegitimate son?

Peter of Burgundy

Louis of Chardonnay

Philip of Cognac

Charles of Champagne

King John had two wives with the same Christian name, both countesses, what was their name?

Eleanor

Isabella

Juliana

Matilda

The first marriage ended in 1199, but how?

She was executed

She died

The marriage was annulled

They were not legally married

Henry III was married to whom?

Eleanor of Provence

Helen of Brittany

Clothilde of Burgundy

Margaret of Anjou

Which royal house did Henry III belong to?

Norman

York

Wessex

Plantagenet

He had two coronation services, there was one at Westminster, where was the other one – four years earlier?

Bristol

Gloucester

Edinburgh

Inverness

How old was Edward II when he died in 1307?

6 1

66

68

72

How many children did Edward II have?

5

8

11

13

Edward, the Black Prince was the father of which King?

Richard I

Richard II

Richard III

Richard IV

Which King enjoyed success at the Battle of Agincourt in 1415?

Henry V

Henry VI

Edward III

Edward IV

In which war was the Battle of Agincourt fought?

Hundred Years War

Thirty Years War

War of the Roses

War of Independence

Who was the father of Thomas of Lancaster, 1st Duke of Clarence, John of Lancaster, 1st Duke of Bedford and Humphrey, 1st Duke of Gloucester, amongst others?

Henry III

Richard II

Richard III

Henry IV

Who was king during the Peasant's Revolt of 1381?

Edward II

Richard II

Henry II

John

Henry V belonged to which royal house?

York

Gloucester

Clarence

Lancaster

Who was Henry V’s wife?

Catherine de Valois

Caroline de Provence

Charlotte of Brittany

Mary of Aquitaine

Where is he buried?

Leeds Castle

Hever Castle

Westminster Abbey

Winchester Cathedral

Who died aged 49 in the Tower of London on 21st May 1471?

Edward IV

Henry VI

Henry III

Edward V

Before becoming king, who held these titles: 4th Duke of York, 7th Earl of March, 5th Earl of Cambridge, 9th Earl of Ulster and 65th Knight of the Order of the Golden Fleece?

Edward IV

Henry VI

Henry III

Edward V

Who was the first Yorkist King of England?

Edward IV

Henry VI

Henry III

Edward V

Who was Richard III married to?

Anne Boleyn

Mary Boleyn

Anne Neville

Cecily Neville

Richard III had two illegitimate children, what were their Christian names?

John and Katherine

Henry and Eleanor

Richard and Isabella

Edward and Elizabeth

What was Richard III's father's name?

Henry Tudor

John of Lancaster

Edward of Wales

Richard of York

Richard III had two elder brothers, one was Edward IV, what was the name of the other one?

Edmund

Henry

Edgar

John

Edward IV was married to whom?

Elizabeth Woodville

Anne Neville

Margaret Beaufort

Margaret Tudor

What were the Christian names of the legendary Princes in the Tower?

Edward and John

Edward and Richard

Edgar and Robert

Edgar and Rupert

Who did Catherine de Valois marry after the king that she was married to died?

Owen Lancaster

Oscar Stuart

Owen Tudor

Oliver York

John of Gaunt married three times, the last time to his mistress, what was her name?

Blanche of Lancaster

Katherine Swynford

Margaret Beaufort

Constance of Castille

How old was John of Gaunt when he died?

58

60

62

64

The Duke of Lancaster is also which of these?

The monarch

The Prince of Wales

The Duke of York

The Duke of Edinburgh

Which King founded the Order of the Garter in 1348?

Edward I

Edward II

Edward III

Edward IV

Who was one of the last medieval women to be given the Order of the Garter, she was also Henry VII's mother?

Elizabeth Woodville

Elizabeth of York

Catherine de Valois

Margaret Beaufort

Which of John of Gaunt's daughter's became Queen of Castille?

Philippa

Catherine

Elizabeth

Joan

Which of John of Gaunt's daughter's became Queen of Portugal?

Philippa

Catherine

Elizabeth

Joan

Who was the first King, in 1066, to use the Tower of London to keep hostile Londoners at bay?

King Harold II

King Harold I

William The Conqueror

William II

Which King had the St Thomas' Tower and the Watergate now known as Traitor's Gate built at the Tower of London?

Edward I

Edward II

Henry II

Henry III

Which year were the "beefeaters" or the Yeoman Warders installed at the Tower of London?

1300

1399

1460

1485

Who acquired Hampton Court Palace in 1236 - before it was a royal palace?

The Knights Hospitallers of St John Jerusalem

The Knights of the Round Table

The Knights of the Garter

The Knights Templar

What did they use it as?

A grange

A stable block

A church

A religious retreat

Windsor Castle has been a family home to the British Royal Family for over how many years?

2000

1500

1000

500

Who chose the site for Windsor Castle?

William II

William the Conqueror

Edward the Confessor

Richard I

Who converted the castle into a palace?

Edward I

Edward II

William the Conqueror

Edward III

Caernafon Castle in Wales was changed from a motte and bailey medieval fortress to a stone castle by which King?

Edward I

Edward II

Edward III

Edward IV

Which cathedral houses a copy of the Magna Carta?

Canterbury

St Paul's, London

Salisbury

Exeter

In the thirteenth century English royal castles were used as gaols and as import/export stores for which of these?

Food, drink and weapons

Livestock

Money, taxes

Jewels

Thomas Beckett, Archbishop of Canterbury, was murdered in Canterbury Cathedral in 1250, he was in dispute with which king?

Henry I

Henry II

Henry III

Henry IV

Which century was the outlaw Robin Hood believed to have been working for the poor?

11th

12th

13th

14th

Which King and his taxes is he rumoured to have been fighting against?

King Stephen

King John

Henry I

Edward I

Who was King at the time of the Black Death in 1346-1353?

Edward II

Edward III

Henry II

Henry III

How many English monarchs have there been since William the Conqueror?

53

45

40

37

Which of these kings has William Shakespeare written about?

Henry IV

Henry V

Henry VI

King John

(Clue: You are looking for more than one!)

To Present Day

Questions

Which male royal played tennis at Wimbledon?

George V

Edward VIII

George VI

Henry, Duke of Gloucester

Which King changed the family name to Windsor?

George VI

George V

Elizabeth II

Edward VII

Queen Victoria was known by which of these before she ascended to the throne?

Princess Victoria of Kent

Princess Victoria of Gloucester

Princess Victoria of Cumberland

Princess Victoria of Cornwall

How many King George's were there between 1714 and 1830?

2

3

4

5

What was Queen Victoria's husband's name?

Albert

George

Edward

Arthur

Edward VII's wife was Princess Alexandra of...where?

Sweden

Norway

Finland

Denmark

George V and Queen Mary had how many daughters?

None

1

2

4

What was George V's elder brother's name?

Albert Victor Christian Edward

Albert William Christian Edward

Edward Victor Christian William

Edward William Christian Victor

Edward VII reigned for how many years?

15

9

7

5

Queen Victoria reigned for how many years?

63

59

50

45

Which royal house did Victoria descend from?

Stuart

Hanover

Plantagenet

Orange

What relation was King William IV to Queen Victoria?

Father

Brother

Son

Uncle

What was King William IV's wife called?

Adelaide

Sydney

Elizabeth

Charlotte

Which country did Edward VII's daughter Maud become queen of?

Sweden

Romania

Denmark

Norway

Was Prince Albert from Saxe Coburg...where?

Anhalt

Wiemar

Gotha

Hanover

How many illegitimate children did William IV have with Dorothy Jordan?

3

6

7

10

How old was William IV when he died?

50

62

71

84

How old was Edward VII when he died?

69

68

67

65

Which of Queen Victoria's daughters was the mother of Kaiser Wilhelm?

Victoria

Beatrice

Alice

Louise

What was George IV known as before he was the king?

The Knight Of The Garter

The King In Waiting

The Prince Consort

The Prince Regent

What was the name of George IV's daughter?

Princess Charlotte

Princess Adelaide

Princess Mary

Princess Elizabeth

What was the name of Queen Victoria's youngest son?

Arthur

Albert

Alfred

Leopold

When did Queen Victoria become Empress of India?

1874

1877

1882

1885

Which of Queen Victoria's granddaughters was Queen of Romania?

Victoria of Hesse and by Rhine

Alexandra of Hesse and by Rhine

Alice of Albany

Marie of Edinbrough

George IV was married to which of these princesses?

Marina of Greece

Elizabeth of Hesse

Caroline of Brunswick

Caroline of Anspach

Which royal had Brighton Pavilion built?

Queen Victoria

George IV

William IV

Edward VII

Of these King George's who reigned for the longest?

George I

George II

George III

George IV

Which of these was the eldest son of George II?

George

Frederick

Charles

Edward

George III and his wife Queen Charlotte had how many children?

14

15

16

17

Which of George III's daughters was given the title The Princess Royal?

Sophia

Charlotte

Mary

Augusta

Which of George III's daughters was given the title Duchess of Gloucester and Edinburgh?

Sophia

Matilda

Mary

Augusta

Which of George III's sons was Duke of Cambridge?

Adolphus

William

Augustus

Ernest

Which of George III's sons died in infancy?

Alfred

William

George

Augustus

William III was married to Mary. She was the daughter of which king?

James II

James III

Charles I

Charles II

Which of George III's children lived the longest?

Charlotte

Mary

Augusta

Sophia

Which royal house did Queen Anne descend from?

Tudor

Hanover

Stuart

Jacobite

What was George III's mother's name?

Augusta

Louise

Charlotte

Sophia

George III's eldest son was known by which name?

George

Frederick

Charles

Edward

Which George was the king when America won independence from Britain?

George I

George II

George III

George IV

Queen Anne was married to Prince George of...where?

Hanover

Greece

Denmark

Sweden

William III was from the House of...where?

Plum

Apricot

Saxe Coburg Gotha

Orange

Queen Anne, Charles II and James II's coronations were on which day?

23rd April – St. George's Day

1st January – New Years Day

25th December – Christmas Day

28th June – Henry VIII's birthday

How old was Queen Anne when she died?

55

44

74

49

James II married twice. What were his wives called?

Mary Seeke and Henrietta FitzJames

Anne Hyde and Mary of Modena

Catherine of Braganza and Mary of Modena

Catherine of Braganza and Mary Seeke

How many of James II’s children became monarchs?

1

2

4

6

James II died in which country?

Scotland

Wales

France

Spain

Charles I was married to which of these princesses?

Catherine of Braganza

Henrietta Maria of France

Sophia of Hanover

Catherine of Aragon

Charles I was executed on 30th January in which year?

1644

1655

1649

1654

How many sons did Charles I have?

3

4

5

6

Charles II had no legitimate issue but he had how many illegitimate children?

At least 30

At least 20

At least 15

At least 25

Where was Charles II buried?

St. Pauls Cathedral

Palace of Westminster

Westminster Abbey

Hampton Court

In 1603 who became King of England?

James VI of Scotland

James IV of Scotland

Phillip II of Spain

Louis XIV of France

Charles I and Charles II belonged to which house?

Tudor

Stuart

Hanover

Plantagenet

Who was James I married to?

Henrietta of France

Catherine de Medici

Elizabeth of Bohemia

Anne of Denmark

Who were Elizabeth I's parents?

Henry VIII and Anne Boleyn

Henry VII and Elizabeth of York

Henry VIII and Katherine Howard

Edward IV and Elizabeth Woodville

How many years did Mary I reign for?

1

3

5

7

How many times did Elizabeth I marry?

3

2

1

0

Edward VI was the son of which monarch?

Henry VII

Queen Anne

Henry VIII

Mary I

Mary I was married to which king?

Philip II of Spain

Louis XIV of France

William of Orange

Philip I of Spain

Lady Jane Grey was queen for how many days in 1553?

16

34

28

9

Lady Jane Grey was executed. Where did she die?

Fotheringay Castle

Tutbury Castle

The Tower of London

The Palace of Whitehall

How old was Edward VI when he died?

22

41

37

15

Which of these wives did Henry VIII divorce?

Catherine of Aragon

Katherine Parr

Anne of Cleves

Jane Seymour

Which of Henry VIII's wives was referred to as the "Flanders Mare?"

Catherine of Aragon

Katherine Parr

Anne of Cleves

Jane Seymour

Henry VII had how many sons?

1

2

3

4

What was Henry VIII known as before he became Prince of Wales?

Duke of Kent

Duke of York

Duke of Clarence

Duke of Norfolk

What were Catherine of Aragon's parent's names?

Ferdinand and Isabella

Felipe and Isabella

Juan Carlos and Sophia

Felipe and Sophia

Henry VII was married to Elizabeth of...where?

Elizabeth of Lancaster

Elizabeth of Scotland

Elizabeth of Aquitaine

Elizabeth of York

How old was Henry VIII when he died?

65

75

55

85

In 1485, how old was Richard III when he fell in battle against Henry VII's supporters?

40

36

33

32

Which battle were they fighting in when he died?

Bosworth Field

Salisbury Plain

Chalk Downs

London Docks

Who became king in 1509?

Henry VII

Henry VIII

Edward VI

Edward V

Which of Henry VIII's sisters was a Queen of Scots?

Margaret

Mary

Elizabeth

Katherine

Which of Henry VIII's sisters was Queen of France?

Margaret

Mary

Elizabeth

Katherine

Who was Henry VII's mother?

Margaret of Anjou

Margaret Beaufort

Katherine Swynford

Mary of Guise

Which wife of Henry VIII's died days after childbirth?

Jane Seymour

Anne of Cleves

Catherine of Aragon

Katherine Parr

Royalty and Politicians

To June 2014 how many Prime Ministers of Great Britain have there been during Elizabeth II's reign?

12

13

14

16

To June 2014 how many US Presidents have there been during Elizabeth II's reign?

11

12

13

14

Which Prime Minister is related to Elizabeth II?

David Cameron

Tony Blair

Sir John Major

Gordon Brown

How many years during Elizabeth II's reign was Winston Churchill Prime Minister of Great Britain?

2

3

4

5

Who was Prime Minister when Princess Diana died?

David Cameron

Sir John Major

Gordon Brown

Tony Blair

Which Prime Minister was Queen Victoria's first?

Melbourne

Palmerston

Disraeli

Gladstone

Which Prime Minister was her last?

Rosebery

Balfour

Churchill

Lloyd George

Which of these men served in Henry VIII's court and helped to arrange the King's marriage to Anne of Cleves?

Thomas Cromwell

Cardinal Wolsley

Thomas Seymour

Thomas Culpepper

Which Stuart monarch was on the throne at the time of the Gunpowder Plot?

Charles I

James I

James II

Charles II

Walpole was the first Prime Minister to live at 10 Downing Street, who was King when he moved in there?

George I

George II

William IV

George V

Which birthday did Queen Elizabeth II celebrate on 21st April 2014?

86

88

90

91

How old was Prince Philip on his birthday, 10th June 2014?

90

91

92

93

Where do the royal family traditionally spend their Christmas holidays?

Windsor

Sandringham

Balmoral

Clarence House

Where do the royal family traditionally spend their summer holidays?

Windsor

Sandringham

Balmoral

Clarence House

On 9th April 2014 Prince Charles and Camilla Duchess of Cornwall had which wedding anniversary?

7 years

8 years

9 years

10 years

Where is their official London residence?

Clarence House

St. James Palace

Buckingham Palace

Kensington Palace

Prince Charles of Wales is also the Duke of which of these?

Devon and Thurso

Cornwall and Rothesay

Cornwall and Inverness

Cornwall and Caithness

What is Camilla, Duchess of Cornwall's daughter's name?

Laura

Louise

Leila

Leanne

What is the name of Camilla's granddaughter who was one of the bridesmaids at the wedding of Prince William and Catherine Middleton in 2011?

Marie

Kimberley

Louise

Eliza

Which year was Prince William born in?

1981

1982

1984

1985

How many great grandchildren does Elizabeth II have? (July 2014)

1

2

3

4

Which day is Prince George of Cambridge's birthday?

June 21st

July 22nd

August 23rd

September 24th

Where did the Duke and Duchess of Cambridge and their son tour in Spring 2014 – Prince George's first tour?

New Zealand and Australia

Canada

United States of America

China

Princess Margaret's son and daughter have which Christian names?

David and Elizabeth

Anthony and Sarah

Anthony and Eliza

David and Sarah

What title is held by this son?

Viscount Severn

Viscount Linley

Viscount Balmoral

Viscount Lascelles

What is his wife's name?

Selina

Sarah

Serena

Sasha

His sister was born on 1st May in which year?

1958

1960

1964

1968

What is the name of her husband?

David Armstrong

Daniel Kent

Daniel Chatto

Timothy Taylor

This couple have two sons. What are their names?

Charles and Mark

Samuel and Arthur

Mark and Alfred

Louis and Edward

Prince Andrew's daughters were born in which years?

1988 and 1990

1989 and 1992

1990 and 1992

1992 and 1993

What are their names?

Beatrice and Elizabeth

Bonnie and Olivia

Michelle and Maria

Beatrice and Eugenie

Where were these daughters born?

Portland Hospital for Women and Children

St. James Palace

St. Mary's Hospital

Buckingham Palace

Which of these ladies is the first female in the line of succession?

Princess Eugenie

Zara Tindall

Princess Beatrice

Lady Louise Mountbatten-Windsor

Princess Anne married Timothy Laurence in 1992 but who was her first husband?

Mark Phillips

Henry Smith

Harry Jones

Peter Marshall

Princess Anne is also known by which title?

The Princess Regal

The Princess Royal

The Princess Charity

The Princess Hope

Princess Anne's daughter, Zara, had a daughter in January 2014, what is her name?

Catherine Elizabeth Tindall

Mia Grace Tindall

Anne Elizabeth Tindall

Marina Grace Tindall

Which honour does Zara hold?

Order of the British Empire

Member of the British Empire

Commander of the British Empire

Order of the Bath

Which sport does she compete in?

Eventing

Tennis

Shooting

Badminton

Zara's brother, Peter, is married to a lady with which name?

Winter

Spring

Summer

Autumn

Which university did Peter and Zara attend?

Oxford

Cambridge

Exeter

St. Andrews

Prince Edward, Earl of Wessex, is married to whom?

Sophia

Sarah

Serena

Sophie

Their son, James, holds which title?

Viscount Linley

Viscount Severn

Viscount Wessex

Viscount Windsor

Their daughter's name is which of these options?

Louise Alice Elizabeth Mary

Alice Louise Elizabeth Mary

Elizabeth Louise Mary Alice

Mary Alice Louise Elizabeth

How old was Prince Edward on his birthday in 2014?

40

50

55

60

Who is Edward, Duke of Kent married to?

Katherine

Louise

Marina

Elizabeth

What is the name of their eldest son?

Edward

William

George

Stephen

What title does this son hold?

Earl of St. Andrews

Earl of Ulster

Earl of Wessex

Duke of Cornwall

What was Edward, Duke of Kent's mother's name?

Marina

Margaret

Mary

Maud

Who is Edward, Duke of Kent's younger brother?

Prince Marcus of Kent

Prince John of Kent

Prince Arthur of Kent

Prince Michael of Kent

What is their sister's name?

Princess Alexandra

Princess Julia

Princess Catherine

Princess Augusta

She was born on Christmas Day 1936, which of these is one of her middle names?

Christina

Christine

Christabel

Holly

Who did she marry in 1963?

Peter Phillips

Angus Ogilvy

Antony Snowdon

George, 7th Earl of Harewood

Which title did Alexandra's husband decline?

Earl

Duke

Viscount

Marquis

What are their children called?

Jack and Elizabeth

Philip and Margaret

John and Katherine

James and Marina

Where is Princess Alexandra's official residence?

St James Palace

Kensington Palace

Windsor Castle

Sandringham House

Edward, Duke of Kent's daughter has which name?

Helena

Hannah

Helen

Harriet

Where did she marry Timothy Taylor?

St. Pauls Cathedral

Crathie Kirk

St George's Chapel, Windsor

Westminster Abbey

Her sons are called which of these names?

Charlie and Chester

Freddie and Franklin

Laurence and Lewis

Columbus and Cassius

What are Prince Michael of Kent's children called?

Frederick and Gabriella

Frederick and Marina

Francis and Gabrielle

Theo and Marina

What are their occupations?

Financial Analyst and Freelance Feature Writer

Financial Analyst and Event Organiser

Event Organiser and Freelance Feature Writer

Chef and Restaurant Owners

What relation is Lord Nicholas Windsor to Edward, Duke of Kent?

Nephew

Son

Father

Uncle

How many sons does Lord Nicholas Windsor have?

One

Four

Three

Two

How many daughters does he have?

None

One

Two

Three

What is Prince Michael of Kent's wife's Christian name?

Marie Christine

Marie Louise

Marie Michelle

Marie Caroline

How many years have they been married?

31

36

45

53

Which country was she born in?

Germany

Hungary

Czech Republic

Austria

What is the name of their first grandchild?

Marina

Maud

Elizabeth

Anne

In the line of succession, who on this list is the highest placed?

The Duke of Gloucester

The Duke of Kent

Earl of Harewood

Lord Frederick Windsor

What is the Christian name of the Duke of Gloucester?

Richard

Robert

Andrew

James

What is his wife's name?

Bridget

Birgitte

Barbara

Katherine

Which country was she born in?

Germany

France

Spain

Denmark

On the 8th July of which year did they marry?

1970

1972

1978

1980

What were the names of the previous Duke and Duchess of Gloucester, Richard's parents?

Henry and Anne

Henry and Jane

Henry and Alice

Henry and Elizabeth

Between 1945-1947 Richard lived in which country when his father was its Governor-General?

Canada

Australia

New Zealand

Mauritius

The current Duke of Gloucester had an elder brother. What was his Christian name?

Walter

Reginald

Henry

William

The current Duke and Duchess of Gloucester have how many children?

Two

Three

Four

Five

What are the daughters called?

Diana and Rebecca

Davina and Rose

Delilah and Rose

Daniella and Rebecca

The son of the Duke of Gloucester holds which title?

Earl of St. Andrews

Earl of Wessex

Earl Snowdon

Earl of Ulster

The grandson of this Duke holds which title?

Lord Gloucester

Lord Culloden

Lord Chancellor

Lord Chamberlain

How many grandchildren do the Duke and Duchess of Gloucester have? (July 2014)

Three

Five

Six

Seven

The Duke and Duchess of Gloucester's official London residence is where?

Buckingham Palace

St. James Palace

Kensington Palace

Clarence House

In which month is the Trooping of the Colour ceremony?

April

May

June

July

In February 2014 Changing The Guard at Buckingham Palace took place when?

Every day

Every odd numbered day

Every even numbered day

There was no change of guard during February

In July of each year there is a Swan Upping ceremony. What is this?

Swans are urged up the River Thames towards London

An annual census of swans that the crown owns on the Thames

A swan race for charity along the Thames

The removal of swans from the River Thames - away from the public.

Which royals receive an annual parliamentary allowance?

The Queen and Prince Philip

The Queen, Prince Philip and their children

The Queen, Prince Phillip, their children and their grandchildren

The Queen, Prince Philip and all members of the royal family who carry out official duties.

At what age do people receive their first birthday card from the monarch?

90 years

100 years

105 years

110 years

Which wedding anniversary is the first one that the monarch sends a card to the couple?

50 years

60 years

70 years

75 years

Who is currently 10th in line to the throne? (July 2014)

James, Viscount Severn

Lady Louise Windsor

Princess Anne

Princess Eugenie

Who is currently 5th in line to the throne? (July 2014)

Prince Henry of Wales

Princess Beatrice

Edward, Earl of Wessex

Andrew, Duke of York

In which year did the Queen sit for her only hologram portrait?

2000

2003

2010

2012

The Queen was the first British monarch to visit which country in 1986?

Indonesia

Grenada

China

Russia

When was the Buckingham Palace website launched?

1993

1997

2000

2002

How many godchildren does Elizabeth II have?

20

25

30

35

A salute of how many guns is given on Prince Philip's birthday?

21

31

41

51

Which flag flies over Buckingham Palace when the Queen is in residence?

The Royal Standard

The Union Flag

White Flag

Commonwealth Flag

What year did Elizabeth II become queen?

1950

1952

1955

1960

What age was Elizabeth II when she became queen?

22

24

25

28

Who was Elizabeth II father?

George VI

Edward VII

George V

Edward VIII

What is the third child of the Queen and Prince Philip called?

Anne

Andrew

Charles

Edward

In November 2013 the Queen and Prince Philip celebrated how many years of marriage?

52

58

60

66

What was the name of Elizabeth II's younger sister?

Catherine Elizabeth

Camilla Rosemary

Alexandra Mary

Margaret Rose

Which of these is one of the Queen's Christian names?

Alexandra

Angela

Helena

Victoria

Which of these is the name of a daughter in law of Elizabeth II?

Zara

Catherine

Camilla

Anne

Which year was the Queen born in?

1923

1926

1929

1930

Which year was Elizabeth II's Golden Jubilee?

2002

2004

2005

2006

What's the name of Elizabeth II's first great grandchild?

Isla

Mia

George

Savannah

What are Prince Edward's Christian names?

Edward Antony Richard Louis

Edward Arthur Philip George

Edward Arthur David Louis

Edward George Mark Charles

What name was the Queen given within the family?

Lilibet

Lily

Lizzy

Lolly

Which breed of dog is Elizabeth II's favourite?

King Charles Spaniel

Golden Retriever

Terrier

Corgi

Answers - Early Monarchy

What was the first king of England's name?

Ǽthelstan

Where did the first king hold the First Council of All England in 931AD?

Colchester

Who is widely acknowledged to have been the first monarch to bestow the title of Prince of Wales on their eldest son?

Edward I

What was name of the King of England who reigned between 978–1013 and 1014–1016?

Æthelred II

Which King sealed the Magna Carta in 1215?

King John I

What does Magna Carta mean in English?

Great Charter

Who was king of England 23 April to 18 October 1016?

Edmund II

What was the name of the King who reigned from 1016 to 1035?

Cnut the Great

What was Harold I known as?

Harold Harefoot

Edward the Confessor was married to whom?

Edith of Wessex

What the names of Edward the Confessor's parents?

Ǽthelred the Unready and Emma of Normandy

Who was the last Anglo-Saxon king of England?

Harold II

In which battle did this king lose the throne?

Battle of Hastings

William II was married how many times?

None

William the Conqueror belonged to which royal dynasty?

Norman

Which date was the Battle of Hastings?

14th October 1066

Who was King of England between 2nd August 1100 and 1st December 1135?

Henry I

Which King followed him?

King Stephen

What was William II popularly known as?

William The Red

How many Kings have there been with the name of Stephen?

One

King Stephen's coronation was on which day?

26th December 1135

What was his wife's name?

Matilda of Boulogne

Eleanor of Aquitaine was married to which king?

Henry II

How many daughters did they have?

Three

Who was Henry II's father?

Geoffrey V, Count of Anjou

Who was the King between 6 July 1189 – 6 April 1199 although he was absent for some of his reign at the Crusades?

Richard I

What was the name of this king's illegitimate son?

Philip of Cognac

King John had two wives with the same Christian name, both countesses, what was their name?

Isabella

The first marriage ended in 1199, but how?

The marriage was annulled

Henry III was married to whom?

Eleanor of Provence

Which royal house did Henry III belong to?

Plantagenet

He had two coronation services, there was one at Westminster, where was the other one – four years earlier?

Gloucester

How old was Edward II when he died in 1307?

68

How many children did Edward II have?

13

Edward, the Black Prince was the father of which King?

Richard II

Which King enjoyed success at the Battle of Agincourt in 1415?

Henry V

In which war was the Battle of Agincourt fought?

Hundred Years War

Who was the father of Thomas of Lancaster, 1st Duke of Clarence, John of Lancaster, 1st Duke of Bedford and Humphrey, 1st Duke of Gloucester, amongst others?

Henry IV

Who was king during the Peasant's Revolt of 1381?

Richard II

Henry V belonged to which royal house?

Lancaster

Who was Henry V's wife?

Catherine de Valois

Where is he buried?

Westminster Abbey

Who died aged 49 in the Tower of London on 21st May 1471?

Henry VI

Before becoming king, who held these titles: 4th Duke of York, 7th Earl of March, 5th Earl of Cambridge, 9th Earl of Ulster and 65th Knight of the Order of the Golden Fleece?

Edward IV

Who was the first Yorkist King of England?

Edward IV

Who was Richard III married to?

Anne Neville

Richard III had two illegitimate children, what were their Christian names?

John and Katherine

What was Richard III's father's name?

Richard of York

Richard III had two elder brothers, one was Edward IV, what was the name of the other one?

Edmund

Edward IV was married to whom?

Elizabeth Woodville

What were the Christian names of the legendary Princes in the Tower?

Edward and Richard

Who did Catherine de Valois marry after the king that she was married to died?

Owen Tudor

John of Gaunt married three times, the last time to his mistress, what was her name?

Katherine Swynford

How old was John of Gaunt when he died?

58

The Duke of Lancaster is also which of these?

The monarch

Which King founded the Order of the Garter in 1348?

Edward III

Who was one of the last medieval women to be given the Order of the Garter, she was also Henry VII's mother?

Margaret Beaufort

Which of John of Gaunt's daughter's became Queen of Castille?

Catherine

Which of John of Gaunt's daughter's became Queen of Portugal?

Philippa

Who was the first King, in 1066, to use the Tower of London to keep hostile Londoners at bay?

William the Conqueror

Which King had the St Thomas' Tower and the Watergate now known as Traitor's Gate built at the Tower of London?

Edward I

Which year were the "beefeaters" or the Yeoman Warders installed at the Tower of London?

1485

Who acquired Hampton Court Palace in 1236 - before it was a royal palace?

The Knights Hospitallers of St John Jerusalem

What did they use it as?

A grange

Windsor Castle has been a family home to the British Royal Family for over how many years?

1000

Who chose the site for Windsor Castle?

William the Conqueror

Who converted Windsor Castle into a palace?

Edward III

Caernafon Castle in Wales was changed from a motte and bailey medieval fortress to a stone castle by which King?

Edward I

Which cathedral houses a copy of the Magna Carta?

Salisbury

In the thirteenth century English royal castles were used as gaols and as import/export stores for which of these?

Food, drink and weapons

Thomas Beckett, Archbishop of Canterbury, was murdered in Canterbury Cathedral in 1250, he was in dispute with which king?

Henry II

Which century was the outlaw Robin Hood believed to have been working for the poor?

13th

Which King and his taxes is he rumoured to have been fighting against?

King John

Who was King at the time of the Black Death in 1346-1353?

Edward III

How many English monarchs have there been since William the Conqueror?

40

Which of these kings has William Shakespeare written about?

Henry IV

Henry V

Henry VI

King John

(The answer is all of them.)

****

Answers – To Present Day

Which male royal played tennis at Wimbledon?

George VI

Which King changed the family name to Windsor?

George V

Queen Victoria was known by which of these before she ascended to the throne?

Princess Victoria of Kent

How many King George's were there between 1714 and 1830?

4

What was Queen Victoria's husband's name?

Albert

Edward VII's wife was Princess Alexandra of...where?

Denmark

George V and Queen Mary had how many daughters?

1

What was George V's elder brother's name?

Albert Victor Christian Edward

Edward VII reigned for how many years?

9

Queen Victoria reigned for how many years?

63

Which royal house did Victoria descend from?

Hanover

What relation was King William IV to Queen Victoria?

Uncle

What was King William IV's wife called?

Adelaide

Which country did Edward VII's daughter Maud become queen of?

Norway

Was Prince Albert from Saxe Coburg...where?

Gotha

How many illegitimate children did William IV have with Dorothy Jordan?

10

How old was William IV when he died?

71

How old was Edward VII when he died?

Which of Queen Victoria's daughters was the mother of Kaiser Wilhelm?

Victoria

What was George IV known as before he was the king?

The Prince Regent

What was the name of George IV's daughter?

Charlotte

What was the name of Queen Victoria's youngest son?

Leopold

When did Queen Victoria become Empress of India?

1877

Which of Queen Victoria's granddaughters was Queen of Romania?

Marie of Edinburgh

George IV was married to which of these princesses?

Caroline of Brunswick

Which royal had Brighton Pavilion built?

George IV

Of these King George's who reigned for the longest?

George III

Which of these was the eldest son of George II?

Frederick

George III and his wife Queen Charlotte had how many children?

15

Which of George III's daughters was given the title The Princess Royal?

Charlotte

Which of George III's daughters was given the title Duchess of Gloucester and Edinburgh?

Mary

Which of George III's sons was Duke of Cambridge?

Adolphus

Which of George III's sons died in infancy?

Alfred

William III was married to Mary. She was the daughter of which king?

James II

Which of George III's children lived the longest?

Mary

Which royal house did Queen Anne descend from?

Stuart

What was George III's mother's name?

Augusta

George III's eldest son was known by which name?

George

Which George was the king when America won independence from Britain?

George III

Queen Anne was married to Prince George of...where?

Denmark

William III was from the House of...where?

Orange

Queen Anne, Charles II and James II's coronations were on which day?

23rd April – St. George's Day

How old was Queen Anne when she died?

49

James II married twice. What were his wives called?

Anne Hyde and Mary of Modena

How many of James II's children became monarchs?

2

James II died in which country?

France

Charles I was married to which of these princesses?

Henrietta Maria of France

Charles I was executed on 30th January in which year?

1649

How many sons did Charles I have?

3

Charles II had no legitimate issue but he had how many illegitimate children?

At least 15

Where was Charles II buried?

Westminster Abbey

In 1603 who became King of England?

James VI of Scotland

Charles I and Charles II belonged to which house?

Stuart

Who was James I married to?

Anne of Denmark

Who were Elizabeth I's parents?

Henry VIII and Anne Boleyn

How many years did Mary I reign for?

5

How many times did Elizabeth I marry?

0

Edward VI was the son of which monarch?

Henry VIII

Mary I was married to which king?

Philip II of Spain

Lady Jane Grey was queen for how many days in 1553?

9

Lady Jane Grey was executed. Where did she die?

The Tower of London

How old was Edward VI when he died?

15

Which of these wives did Henry VIII divorce?

Anne of Cleves

Which of Henry VIII's wives was referred to as the "Flanders Mare?"

Anne of Cleves

Henry VII had how many sons?

3

What was Henry VIII known as before he became Prince of Wales?

Duke of York

What were Catherine of Aragon's parent's names?

Ferdinand and Isabella

Henry VII was married to Elizabeth of...where?

Elizabeth of York

How old was Henry VIII when he died?

55

In 1485, how old was Richard III when he fell in battle against Henry VII's supporters?

32

Which battle were they fighting in when he died?

Bosworth Field

Who became king in 1509?

Henry VIII

Which of Henry VIII's sisters was a Queen of Scots?

Margaret

Which of Henry VIII's sisters was Queen of France?

Mary

Who was Henry VII's mother?

Margaret Beaufort

Which wife of Henry VIII's died days after childbirth and was said to have been his favourite wife?

Jane Seymour

Royalty and Politicians

To June 2014 how many Prime Ministers of Great Britain have there been during Elizabeth II's reign?

12

To June 2014 how many US Presidents have there been during Elizabeth II's reign?

12

Which Prime Minister is related to Elizabeth II?

David Cameron

How many years during Elizabeth II's reign was Winston Churchill Prime Minister of Great Britain?

3

Who was Prime Minister when Princess Diana died?

Tony Blair

Which Prime Minister was Queen Victoria's first?

Melbourne

Which Prime Minister was her last?

Rosebery

Which of these men served in Henry VIII's court and helped to arrange the King's marriage to Anne of Cleves?

Thomas Cromwell

Which Stuart monarch was on the throne at the time of the Gunpowder Plot?

James I

Walpole was the first Prime Minister to live at 10 Downing Street, who was the king when he moved in there?

George II

Which birthday did Queen Elizabeth II celebrate on 21st April 2014?

88

How old was Prince Philip on his birthday, 10th June 2014?

93

Where do the royal family traditionally spend their Christmas holidays?

Sandringham

Where do the royal family traditionally spend their summer holidays?

Balmoral

On 9th April 2014 Prince Charles and Camilla Duchess of Cornwall had which wedding anniversary?

9 years

Where is their official London residence?

Clarence House

Prince Charles of Wales is also the Duke of which of these?

Cornwall and Rothesay

What is Camilla, Duchess of Cornwall's daughter's name?

Laura

What is the name of Camilla's granddaughter who was one of the bridesmaids at the wedding of Prince William and Catherine Middleton in 2011?

Eliza

Which year was Prince William born in?

1982

How many great grandchildren does Elizabeth II have? (July 2014)

4

Which day is Prince George of Cambridge's birthday?

July 22nd

Where did the Duke and Duchess of Cambridge and their son tour in Spring 2014 – Prince George's first tour?

New Zealand and Australia

Princess Margaret's son and daughter have which Christian names?

David and Sarah

What title is held by this son?

Viscount Linley

What is his wife's name?

Serena

His sister was born on 1st May in which year?

1964

What is the name of her husband?

Daniel Chatto

This couple have two sons. What are their names?

Samuel and Arthur

Prince Andrew's daughters were born in which years?

1988 and 1990

What are their names?

Beatrice and Eugenie

Where were these daughters born?

Portland Hospital for Women and Children

Which of these ladies is the first female in the line of succession?

Princess Beatrice

Princess Anne married Timothy Laurence in 1992 but who was her first husband?

Mark Phillips

Princess Anne is also known by which title?

The Princess Royal

Princess Anne's daughter, Zara, had a daughter in January 2014, what is her name?

Mia Grace Tindall

Which honour does Zara hold?

Member of the British Empire

Which sport does she compete in?

Eventing

Zara's brother, Peter, is married to a lady with which name?

Autumn

Which university did Peter and Zara attend?

Exeter

Prince Edward, Earl of Wessex, is married to whom?

Sophie

Their son, James, holds which title?

Viscount Severn

Their daughter's name is which of these options?

Louise Alice Elizabeth Mary

How old was Prince Edward on his birthday in 2014?

50

Who is Edward, Duke of Kent married to?

Katherine

What is the name of their eldest son?

George

What title does this son hold?

Earl of St. Andrews

What was Edward, Duke of Kent's mother's name?

Marina

Who is Edward, Duke of Kent's younger brother?

Prince Michael of Kent

What is their sister's name?

Princess Alexandra

She was born on Christmas Day 1936, which of these is one of her middle names?

Christabel

Who did she marry in 1963?

Angus Ogilvy

Which title did Alexandra's husband decline?

Earl

What are their children called?

James and Marina

Where is Princess Alexandra's official residence?

St James Palace

Edward, Duke of Kent's daughter has which name?

Helen

Where did she marry Timothy Taylor?

St George's Chapel, Windsor

Her sons are called which of these names?

Columbus and Cassius

What are Prince Michael of Kent's children called?

Frederick and Gabriella

What are their occupations?

Financial Analyst and Freelance Feature Writer

What relation is Lord Nicholas Windsor to Edward, Duke of Kent?

Son

How many sons does Lord Nicholas Windsor have?

Three

How many daughters does he have?

None

What is Prince Michael of Kent's wife's Christian name?

Marie Christine

How many years have they been married? (2014)

36

Which country was she born in?

Czech Republic

What is the name of their first grandchild?

Maud

In the line of succession, who on this list is the highest placed?

The Duke of Gloucester

What is the Christian name of the Duke of Gloucester?

Richard

What is his wife's name?

Birgitte

Which country was she born in?

Denmark

On the 8th July of which year did they marry?

1972

What were the names of the previous Duke and Duchess of Gloucester, Richard's parents?

Henry and Alice

Between 1945-1947 Richard lived in which country when his father was its Governor-General?

Australia

The current Duke of Gloucester had an elder brother. What was his Christian name?

William

The current Duke and Duchess of Gloucester have how many children?

Three

What are the daughters called?

Davina and Rose

The son of the Duke of Gloucester holds which title?

Earl of Ulster

The grandson of this Duke holds which title?

Lord Culloden

How many grandchildren do the Duke and Duchess of Gloucester have? (July 2014)

Six

The Duke and Duchess of Gloucester's official London residence is where?

Kensington Palace

In which month is the Trooping of the Colour ceremony?

June

In February 2014 Changing The Guard at Buckingham Palace took place when?

Every even numbered day

In July of each year there is a Swan Upping ceremony. What is this?

An annual census of swans that the crown owns on the Thames

Which royals receive an annual parliamentary allowance?

The Queen and Prince Philip

At what age do people receive their first birthday card from the monarch?

100 years

Which wedding anniversary is the first one that the monarch sends a card to the couple?

60 years

Who is currently 10th in line to the throne? (July 2014)

Lady Louise Mountbatten - Windsor

Who is currently 5th in line to the throne? (July 2014)

Andrew, Duke of York

In which year did the Queen sit for her only hologram portrait?

2003

The Queen was the first British monarch to visit which country in 1986?

China

When was the Buckingham Palace website launched?

1997

How many godchildren does Elizabeth II have?

30

A salute of how many guns is given on Prince Philip's birthday?

41

Which flag flies over Buckingham Palace when the Queen is in residence?

The Royal Standard

What year did Elizabeth II become queen?

1952

What age was Elizabeth II when she became queen?

25

Who was Elizabeth II's father?

George VI

What is the third child of the Queen and Prince Philip called?

Andrew

In November 2013 the Queen and Prince Philip celebrated how many years of marriage?

66

What was the name of Elizabeth II's younger sister?

Margaret Rose

Which of these is one of the Queen's Christian names?

Alexandra

Which of these is the name of a daughter in law of Elizabeth II?

Camilla

Which year was the Queen born in?

1926

Which year was Elizabeth II's Golden Jubilee?

2002

What's the name of Elizabeth II's first great grandchild?

Savannah

What are Prince Edward's Christian names?

Edward Antony Richard Louis

What name was the Queen given within the family?

Lilibet

Which breed of dog is Elizabeth II's favourite?

Corgi

Thank you for reading this book.

*There are more of my books available on Amazon and my short stories are available on **www.alfiedog.com** and a selection of my children's stories have been published on **www.childrens-stories.net***

I also have a positive blog about O.C.D.,P.T.S.D and my writing: joannehayle.wordpress.com

If you are interested, please have a read!

Thank you

Joanne.

12339891R00094

Printed in Great Britain
by Amazon